5 progressive levels

Rules of the game :

Using the operations +, -, x and /, find the required result.
Use <u>all</u> the hours and minutes figures, either separated or grouped.

Examples :

06:36 Find 30	*36 - 06 = 30*

10:32 Find 50	*3 + 2 = 5 5 x 10 = 50*

22:41 Find 10	*2 x 4 = 8 8 + 2 = 10 10 x 1 = 10*

23:56 Find 9	*2 + 5 = 7 6/3 = 2 7 + 2 = 9*

The 24-hour clock gives more possibilities

Mental Clock

5 progressive levels

Marc Riviere

iUniverse, Inc.
Bloomington

Mental Clock
The new mental game!

iUniverse books may be ordered through booksellers or by contacting:

iUniverse
1663 Liberty Drive
Bloomington, IN 47403
www.iuniverse.com
1-800-Authors (1-800-288-4677)

Because of the dynamic nature of the Internet, any web addresses or links contained in this book may have changed since publication and may no longer be valid. The views expressed in this work are solely those of the author and do not necessarily reflect the views of the publisher, and the publisher hereby disclaims any responsibility for them.

Any people depicted in stock imagery provided by Thinkstock are models, and such images are being used for illustrative purposes only.

Certain stock imagery © Thinkstock.

ISBN: 978-1-4502-9253-5 (sc)
ISBN: 978-1-4502-9488-1 (ebook)

Printed in the United States of America

iUniverse rev. date: 02/04/2011

1 - 2 - 3 - 4 - 5

| 07:20 | |
| Find 20 | |

| 10:10 | |
| Find 10 | |

| 18:20 | |
| Find 10 | |

| 03:37 | |
| Find 10 | |

| 10:39 | |
| Find 10 | |

| 17:47 | |
| Find 30 | |

19:50	
Find 40	

09:45	
Find 10	

07:38	
Find 10	

05:29	
Find 10	

08:48	
Find 40	

14:16	
Find 20	

16:37 Find 30	
20:32 Find 30	
12:47 Find 50	
19:09 Find 10	
05:52 Find 10	
19:58 Find 50	

21:34
Find 20

14:56
Find 0

02:18
Find 20

06:10
Find 60

13:52
Find 50

06:40
Find 10

20:02 Find 10	
20:08 Find 10	
07:23 Find 30	
13:27 Find 30	
12:34 Find 0	
05:49 Find 20	

05:28
Find 40

22:12
Find 10

18:32
Find 0

05:16
Find 80

14:38
Find 0

06:46
Find 10

18:18 Find 10	

15:51 Find 20	

15:36 Find 30	

14:10 Find 40	

01:49 Find 50	

05:38 Find 40	

04:28
Find 10

03:33
Find 30

01:56
Find 10

14:45
Find 50

22:19
Find 10

14:20
Find 80

20:52
Find 23

17:57
Find 49

15:18
Find 33

17:32
Find 2

22:17
Find 9

20:53
Find 6

21:12 Find 18	
17:53 Find 36	
12:56 Find 53	
21:46 Find 6	
12:44 Find 22	
12:58 Find 1	

12:49

Find 0

Find 10

Find 20

Find 30

Find 40

Find 50

Find 60

Find 70

Find 80

Find 90

Find 100

Mental Clock

1 - **2** - 3 - 4 - 5

| 16:52 | |
| Find 40 | |

| 20:37 | |
| Find 80 | |

| 15:17 | |
| Find 40 | |

| 14:25 | |
| Find 100 | |

| 20:28 | |
| Find 20 | |

| 02:29 | |
| Find 10 | |

13:54
Find 40

15:49
Find 50

05:19
Find 50

19:44
Find 20

17:42
Find 30

13:24
Find 10

05:55
Find 20

23: 17
Find 20

17:39
Find 60

15:37
Find 0

15: 10
Find 60

23:42
Find 90

12:46 Find 90	
20:56 Find 40	
12:27 Find 70	
14:59 Find 40	
10:28 Find 40	
16:49 Find 10	

19:37 Find 0	
15:49 Find 90	
21:56 Find 60	
10:51 Find 10	
22:21 Find 10	
18:48 Find 10	

14:36 Find 10	
16:57 Find 70	
14:56 Find 30	
14:47 Find 40	
18:48 Find 20	
12:34 Find 60	

14: 19 Find 80	

12 : 52 Find 10	

22 : 45 Find 40	

18 : 42 Find 80	

19 : 24 Find 60	

14: 12 Find 10	

14:43
Find 20

18:36
Find 0

20:31
Find 40

23:44
Find 40

07:35
Find 20

08:52
Find 20

15:28
Find 41

14:55
Find 34

18:49
Find 18

14: 16
Find 5

21:36
Find 26

11:57
Find 23

17:44	
Find 33	

21:29	
Find 45	

18:52	
Find 49	

23:56	
Find 9	

10:44	
Find 36	

12:58	
Find 7	

13:55

Find 0	
Find 10	
Find 20	
Find 30	
Find 40	
Find 50	
Find 60	
Find 70	
Find 80	
Find 90	
Find 100	

Mental Clock

Bonus

1 - 2 - **3** - 4 - 5

18:43 Find 60	

15:47 Find 60	

16:46 Find 100	

14:23 Find 30	

22:48 Find 50	

15:37 Find 70	

16:24 Find 50	
14:29 Find 90	
22:37 Find 30	
17:13 Find 90	
23:46 Find 60	
15:46 Find 90	

2 1:58	
Find 70	

17: 15	
Find 70	

23:25	
Find 50	

13:25	
Find 40	

23:27	
Find 30	

18: 15	
Find 20	

23:44 Find 80	
18:58 Find 20	
23:19 Find 60	
15:27 Find 80	
14:33 Find 40	
19:36 Find 80	

16:29

Find 90

23:49

Find 90

07:59

Find 80

16:29

Find 30

17:26

Find 100

19:42

Find 90

16:39 Find 60	
22:55 Find 20	
14:54 Find 100	
11:53 Find 30	
16:52 Find 50	
19:14 Find 10	

23:54 Find 60	
15:58 Find 60	
19:27 Find 80	
13:26 Find 90	
22:29 Find 40	
13:47 Find 80	

18:37

Find 60

21:49

Find 80

14:15

Find 40

15:26

Find 70

13:57

Find 100

21:58

Find 90

12:37 Find 41	
22:49 Find 74	
17:38 Find 14	
15:46 Find 53	
21:48 Find 92	
12:43 Find 23	

| 19:54 | |
| Find 82 | |

| 13:49 | |
| Find 65 | |

| 19:28 | |
| Find 7 | |

| 19:43 | |
| Find 29 | |

| 17:16 | |
| Find 44 | |

| 12:28 | |
| Find 94 | |

16:59

Find 0

Find 10

Find 20

Find 30

Find 40

Find 50

Find 60

Find 70

Find 80

Find 90

Find 100

Mental Clock

1 - 2 - 3 - **4** - 5

13:39
Find 80

17:46
Find 30

15:57
Find 20

23:56
Find 80

18:17
Find 30

16:49
Find 60

22:55
Find 60

19:16
Find 30

23:35
Find 90

16:28
Find 90

23:58
Find 60

18:57
Find 80

23:53
Find 90

16: 17
Find 20

15:53
Find 70

17: 18
Find 30

14:38
Find 100

19:33
Find 80

15:53 Find 80	
23:58 Find 50	
16:47 Find 30	
19:47 Find 80	
23:38 Find 20	
18:59 Find 90	

21:48 Find 60	
17:58 Find 70	
23:46 Find 70	
18:56 Find 70	
17:27 Find 100	
19:49 Find 90	

17:58

Find 90

16:38

Find 20

18:28

Find 30

23:38

Find 30

15:35

Find 70

18:57

Find 70

17:29
Find 30

19:27
Find 30

22:59
Find 80

14:46
Find 100

16:58
Find 70

14:28
Find 60

17:59 Find 80	
18:16 Find 20	
22:56 Find 70	
18:26 Find 90	
23:58 Find 70	
19:49 Find 20	

17:47
Find 57

23:59
Find 75

16:53
Find 96

17:49
Find 16

18:29
Find 51

19:46
Find 75

22:38 Find 22	

19:59 Find 91	

22:46 Find 33	

16:47 Find 51	

19:57 Find 79	

16:59 Find 6	

18:25

Find 0	
Find 10	
Find 20	
Find 30	
Find 40	
Find 50	
Find 60	
Find 70	
Find 80	
Find 90	
Find 100	

Mental Clock

Bonus

1 - 2 - 3 - 4 - **5**

Out of time

67:62 Find 90	

69:87 Find 30	

32:85 Find 70	

27:94 Find 100	

37:78 Find 50	

75:96 Find 100	

88:27	
Find 90	

63:84	
Find 60	

56:94	
Find 30	

96:47	
Find 70	

78:28	
Find 90	

93:95	
Find 90	

76:57 Find 90	

67:89 Find 30	

86:34 Find 80	

84:96 Find 60	

69:88 Find 20	

94:66 Find 10	

86:96 Find 100	
94:89 Find 50	
27:88 Find 30	
86:47 Find 60	
86:67 Find 90	
88:27 Find 40	

34:67 Find 90	

36:89 Find 40	

85:57 Find 40	

46:78 Find 100	

76:67 Find 90	

56:89 Find 60	

59:47 Find 20	
76:75 Find 100	
69:64 Find 90	
64:78 Find 100	
79:42 Find 100	
65:45 Find 90	

64:68 Find 100	

86:67 Find 70	

75:49 Find 20	

85:32 Find 70	

67:37 Find 60	

94:89 Find 80	

86 : 49	
Find 60	

97 : 77	
Find 10	

69 : 75	
Find 100	

67 : 57	
Find 100	

88 : 62	
Find 30	

86 : 96	
Find 20	

| 67:79 | |
| Find 89 | |

| 98:76 | |
| Find 19 | |

| 86:46 | |
| Find 17 | |

| 63:99 | |
| Find 25 | |

| 78:77 | |
| Find 98 | |

| 89:99 | |
| Find 7 | |

79:76
Find 82

66:78
Find 91

49:69
Find 54

76:98
Find 89

68:89
Find 96

99:99
Find 8

21:59

Find 0

Find 10

Find 20

Find 30

Find 40

Find 50

Find 60

Find 70

Find 80

Find 90

Find 100

Mental Clock

Bonus

Solutions

01 : 49			1+49	=	50
01 : 56		5-1=4	4+6	=	10
02 : 18			2+18	=	20
02 : 29		2/2=1	1+9	=	10
03 : 33			33-3	=	30
03 : 37	0x3=0	0+3=3	3+7	=	10
04 : 28	0x4=0	0+2=2	2+8	=	10
05 : 16			5x16	=	80
05 : 19		1+9=10	5x10	=	50
05 : 28	0x2=0	0+5=5	5x8	=	40
05 : 29	0x9=0	0+5=5	5x2	=	10
05 : 38	0x3=0	0+5=5	5x8	=	40
05 : 49	0x9=0	0+5=5	5x4	=	20
05 : 52	0x2=0	0+5=5	5+5	=	10
05 : 55		5x5=25	25-5	=	20
06 : 10			6x10	=	60
06 : 40		6+4=10	10+0	=	10
06 : 46	0x6=0	0+4=4	4+6	=	10
07 : 20		0x7=0	0+20	=	20
07 : 23			7+23	=	30
07 : 35		7-3=4	4x5	=	20
07 : 38	0x8=0	0+7=7	7+3	=	10
07 : 59		7+9=16	16x5	=	80
08 : 48			48-8	=	40
08 : 52		8x5=40	40/2	=	20
09 : 45		9+5=14	14-4	=	10
10 : 10		10x1=10	10+0	=	10
10 : 28		10/2=5	5x8	=	40
10 : 39	1+9=10	0x3=0	10+0	=	10
10 : 44		10x4=40	40-4	=	36
10 : 51	1+0=1	1+1=2	2x5	=	10
11 : 53	1+1=2	2x5=10	10x3	=	30
11 : 57		11+5=16	16+7	=	23
12 : 27		12-2=10	10x7	=	70
12 : 28		12x8=96	96-2	=	94
12 : 34	1+2=3	3-3=0	0x4	=	0
12 : 34		12+3=15	15x4	=	60
12 : 37	3x7=21	2x21=42	42-1	=	41
12 : 43	2x4=8	8x3=24	24-1	=	23
12 : 44		1x2=2	44/2	=	22
12 : 46		46-1=45	45x2	=	90
12 : 47		2+1=3	3+47	=	50
12 : 49	9-1=8	8/2=4	4-4	=	0
12 : 49	1+2=3	4-3=1	1+9	=	10
12 : 49	1+9=10	4-2=2	10x2	=	20
12 : 49	9-1=8	8x4=32	32-2	=	30
12 : 49	2-1=1	1+9=10	10x4	=	40
12 : 49		2-1=1	1+49	=	50
12 : 49	1+9=10	2+4=6	10x6	=	60
12 : 49	4x9=36	36-1=35	35x2	=	70
12 : 49	1+9=10	10x2=20	20x4	=	80
12 : 49	1+4=5	5x2=10	10x9	=	90
12 : 49		1+49=50	50x2	=	100
12 : 52	1+2=3	3+5=8	8+2	=	10
12 : 56		56-1=55	55-2	=	53
12 : 58		5+8=13	13-12	=	1
12 : 58	1+8=9	9+5=14	14/2	=	7
13 : 24	1+3=4	4+2=6	6+4	=	10
13 : 25	1+3=4	4x2=8	8x5	=	40
13 : 26		13+2=15	15x6	=	90
13 : 27		1x3=3	3+27	=	30
13 : 39	3x3=9	9x9=81	81-1	=	80
13 : 47		13+7=20	20x4	=	80
13 : 49		9-4=5	13x5	=	65
13 : 52		3-1=2	52-2	=	50
13 : 54	1+3=4	4+4=8	8x5	=	40
13 : 55		5-5=0	13x0	=	0
13 : 55	1x3=3	5-3=2	2x5	=	10
13 : 55	1x3=3	3x5=15	15+5	=	20
13 : 55	1x3=3	5+5=10	3x10	=	30
13 : 55	1x3=3	3+5=8	8x5	=	40
13 : 55	3-1=2	2x5=10	10x5	=	50
13 : 55		13x5=65	65-5	=	60
13 : 55		13x5=65	65+5	=	70
13 : 55	3x5=15	1+15=16	16x5	=	80
13 : 55		13+5=18	18x5	=	90
13 : 55	1+3=4	4x5=20	20x5	=	100
13 : 57		13+7=20	20x5	=	100
14 : 10		1x4=4	4x10	=	40
14 : 12	1+4=5	5x1=5	5x2	=	10
14 : 15	1+1=2	2x4=8	8x5	=	40
14 : 16		16/4=4	1+4	=	5
14 : 16		1x4=4	4+16	=	20
14 : 19		1+19=20	20x4	=	80
14 : 20		1x4=4	4x20	=	80
14 : 23	1+4=5	5x2=10	10x3	=	30
14 : 25		1x4=4	4x25	=	100
14 : 28	2x8=16	16-1=15	15x4	=	60
14 : 29	1+4=5	5x2=10	10x9	=	90

14 : 33	3x3=9	1+9=10	10x4	=	40
14 : 36	1+3=4	4x4=16	16-6	=	10
14 : 38	4-1=3	3-3=0	0x8	=	0
14 : 38	3x8=24	1+24=25	25x4	=	100
14 : 43	1+3=4	4x4=16	16+4	=	20
14 : 45		1+4=5	5+45	=	50
14 : 46	4x6=24	1+24=25	25x4	=	100
14 : 47	4-1=3	3+7=10	10x4	=	40
14 : 54	1+4=5	5x4=20	20x5	=	100
14 : 55	1+5=6	6x5=30	30+4	=	34
14 : 56	1+4=5	5-5=0	0x6	=	0
14 : 56	4x6=24	1+24=25	25+5	=	30
14 : 59	1+4=5	5x9=45	45-5	=	40
15 : 10		1+5=6	6x10	=	60
15 : 17	1x5=5	1+7=8	5x8	=	40
15 : 18			15+18	=	33
15 : 26	1+6=7	7x5=35	35x2	=	70
15 : 27	1+7=8	8x5=40	40x2	=	80
15 : 28	2-1=1	5x8=40	1+40	=	41
15 : 35	5x3=15	15-1=14	14x5	=	70
15 : 36		1+5=6	36-6	=	30
15 : 37	5-1=4	4+3=7	7-7	=	0
15 : 37	3-1=2	2x5=10	10x7	=	70
15 : 46	5+4=9	9x6=54	54-1	=	53
15 : 46	4-1=3	5x6=30	3x30	=	90
15 : 47	1+4=5	5+7=12	12x5	=	60
15 : 49	1+4=5	5x9=45	45+5	=	50
15 : 49	1+5=6	6+4=10	10x9	=	90
15 : 51		15+5=20	20x1	=	20
15 : 53	5x3=15	15-1=14	14x5	=	70
15 : 53	5x3=15	1+15=16	16x5	=	80
15 : 57		5x7=35	35-15	=	20
15 : 58	5-1=4	4+8=12	12x5	=	60
16 : 17	1+1=2	2x7=14	14+6	=	20
16 : 24	6x4=24	1+24=25	25x2	=	50
16 : 28	2x8=16	16-1=15	15x6	=	90
16 : 29	1x6=6	6+9=15	15x2	=	30
16 : 29	6-1=5	5x2=10	10x9	=	90
16 : 37		1+6=7	37-7	=	30
16 : 38	3-1=2	2x6=12	12+8	=	20
16 : 39	1+6=7	7x9=63	63-3	=	60
16 : 46		16x6=96	96+4	=	100
16 : 47	7-1=6	6x4=24	24+6	=	30
16 : 47	6+7=13	13x4=52	52-1	=	51
16 : 49	6-1=5	5-4=1	1+9	=	10
16 : 49	1x6=6	6+9=15	15x4	=	60
16 : 52	1x6=6	6+2=8	8x5	=	40
16 : 52	6-1=5	5x5=25	25x2	=	50
16 : 53	5x3=15	1+15=16	16x6	=	96
16 : 57	6-1=5	5+5=10	10x7	=	70
16 : 58	1x6=6	6+8=14	14x5	=	70
16 : 59	5-1=4	4x9=36	36/6	=	6
16 : 59	6-1=5	5-5=0	0x9	=	0
16 : 59	1x6=6	6-5=1	1+9	=	10
16 : 59		9-5=4	16+4	=	20
16 : 59		16+5=21	21+9	=	30
16 : 59	6-1=5	5x9=45	45-5	=	40
16 : 59	6-1=5	5x9=45	45+5	=	50
16 : 59	6x9=54	1+54=55	55+5	=	60
16 : 59	6-1=5	5+9=14	14x5	=	70
16 : 59	1+9=10	10+6=16	16x5	=	80
16 : 59	6-1=5	5+5=10	10x9	=	90
16 : 59	6+5=11	11x9=99	1+99	=	100
17 : 13		7x13=91	91-1	=	90
17 : 15	1+1=2	2x5=10	10x7	=	70
17 : 16	1+1=2	7x6=42	2+42	=	44
17 : 18	1+1=2	7+8=15	2x15	=	30
17 : 26		17x6=102	102-2	=	100
17 : 27	7x7=49	1+49=50	50x2	=	100
17 : 29	7-1=6	6+9=15	15x2	=	30
17 : 32	1x7=7	7-2=5	5-3	=	2
17 : 38	1+3=4	8/4=2	2x7	=	14
17 : 39	1x7=7	7x9=63	63-3	=	60
17 : 42		17x2=34	34-4	=	30
17 : 44	1+4=5	7x4=28	5+28	=	33
17 : 46	7-1=6	6x4=24	24+6	=	30
17 : 47			47-17	=	30
17 : 47	7+7=14	14x4=56	1+56	=	57
17 : 49	7x9=63	1+63=64	64/4	=	16
17 : 53			53-17	=	36
17 : 57		57-7=50	50-1	=	49
17 : 58	7-1=6	6+8=14	14x5	=	70
17 : 58	5+8=13	7x13=91	91-1	=	90
17 : 59	1x7=7	7+9=16	16x5	=	80
18 : 15	1+1=2	8/2=4	4x5	=	20
18 : 16	1+1=2	2x6=12	12+8	=	20
18 : 17	1+1=2	8+7=15	2x15	=	30
18 : 18		18x1=18	18-8	=	10
18 : 20	1x8=8	8+2=10	10+0	=	10

18	: 25	8-1=7	7-2=5	5-5	=	0
18	: 25	8-1=7	7-2=5	5+5	=	10
18	: 25	1x8=8	8/2=4	4x5	=	20
18	: 25	1x8=8	8-2=6	6x5	=	30
18	: 25	2-1=1	1x8=8	8x5	=	40
18	: 25	1x8=8	8+2=10	10x5	=	50
18	: 25	1+5=6	8+2=10	6x10	=	60
18	: 25	8-1=7	7x5=35	35x2	=	70
18	: 25		18-2=16	16x5	=	80
18	: 25	1+8=9	9x5=45	45x2	=	90
18	: 25		18+2=20	20x5	=	100
18	: 26	8x2=16	16-1=15	15x6	=	90
18	: 28	8-1=7	7+8=15	15x2	=	30
18	: 29	1+2=3	8+9=17	3x17	=	51
18	: 32	3-1=2	2-2=0	0x8	=	0
18	: 36		3x6=18	18-18	=	0
18	: 37	1+8=9	9x7=63	63-3	=	60
18	: 42		18+2=20	20x4	=	80
18	: 43		18-3=15	15x4	=	60
18	: 48	1x8=8	8/4=2	2+8	=	10
18	: 48		8/4=2	18+2	=	20
18	: 49	1x8=8	8/4=2	2x9	=	18
18	: 52	8+2=10	10x5=50	50-1	=	49
18	: 56	1x8=8	8+6=14	14x5	=	70
18	: 57	8-1=7	7+7=14	14x5	=	70
18	: 57	1+8=9	9+7=16	16x5	=	80
18	: 58	8-1=7	7+5=12	12+8	=	20
18	: 59	1+9=10	10+8=18	18x5	=	90
19	: 09			19-9	=	10
19	: 14	1+1=2	9-4=5	2x5	=	10
19	: 16	1+1=2	9+6=15	2x15	=	30
19	: 24	1+9=10	2+4=6	10x6	=	60
19	: 27	9-1=8	8+7=15	15x2	=	30
19	: 27	2+7=9	9x9=81	81-1	=	80
19	: 28	1x9=9	2x8=16	16-9	=	7
19	: 33	9x3=27	27x3=81	81-1	=	80
19	: 36	3+6=9	9x9=81	81-1	=	80
19	: 37	1+9=10	3+7=10	10-10	=	0
19	: 42	1+4=5	5x9=45	45x2	=	90
19	: 43	9-1=8	8x4=32	32-3	=	29
19	: 44		4/4=1	19+1	=	20
19	: 46	1+4=5	9+6=15	5x15	=	75
19	: 47	1+4=5	9+7=16	5x16	=	80
19	: 49	9x9=81	81-1=80	80/4	=	20
19	: 49	1+4=5	9+9=18	5x18	=	90
19	: 50		50-1=49	49-9	=	40
19	: 54	5+4=9	9x9=81	1+81	=	82
19	: 57	9+7=16	16x5=80	80-1	=	79
19	: 58		9-1=8	58-8	=	50
19	: 59	9+9=18	18x5=90	1+90	=	91
20	: 02			20/2	=	10
20	: 08		2+0=2	2+8	=	10
20	: 28	2+0=2	2+8=10	10x2	=	20
20	: 31		3-1=2	20x2	=	40
20	: 32		2+0=2	32-2	=	30
20	: 37		7-3=4	20x4	=	80
20	: 52		20+5=25	25-2	=	23
20	: 53	2+0=2	5-2=3	3+3	=	6
20	: 56	2+0=2	2+6=8	8x5	=	40
21	: 12		21-1=20	20-2	=	18
21	: 29	2+1=3	3+2=5	5x9	=	45
21	: 34		21+3=24	24-4	=	20
21	: 36	1+3=4	4x6=24	2+24	=	26
21	: 46	2+1=3	4-3=1	1x6	=	6
21	: 48	2x8=16	16-1=15	15x4	=	60
21	: 48		21x4=84	84+8	=	92
21	: 49	2x4=8	1+9=10	8x10	=	80
21	: 56	2x1=2	2x5=10	10x6	=	60
21	: 58	2x5=10	8-1=7	10x7	=	70
21	: 58	2x5=10	1+8=9	10x9	=	90
21	: 59	2x5=10	10-1=9	9-9	=	0
21	: 59	1+9=10	10/2=5	5+5	=	10
21	: 59	2x5=10	10+9=19	19+1	=	20
21	: 59		1+59=60	60/2	=	30
21	: 59	2-1=1	9-1=8	8x5	=	40
21	: 59	2-1=1	1+9=10	10x5	=	50
21	: 59		2-1=1	1+59	=	60
21	: 59	2+5=7	1+9=10	7x10	=	70
21	: 59			21+59	=	80
21	: 59	2x1=2	2x5=10	10x9	=	90
21	: 59	2x5=10	1+9=10	10x10	=	100
22	: 12			22-12	=	10
22	: 17	2-1=1	1x2=2	2+7	=	9
22	: 19	2-2=0	0+1=1	1+9	=	10
22	: 21		22/2=11	11-1	=	10
22	: 29		2x9=18	22+18	=	40
22	: 37	2x3=6	7-2=5	6x5	=	30
22	: 38	2x3=6	2x8=16	6+16	=	22
22	: 45	2+2=4	4+4=8	8x5	=	40

22	: 46		22x6=132	132/4	= 33
22	: 48	2+4=6	6x8=48	48+2	= 50
22	: 49	4x9=36	2x36=72	72+2	= 74
22	: 55	2/2=1	5-1=4	4x5	= 20
22	: 55	2x5=10	10+2=12	12x5	= 60
22	: 56	2x6=12	12+2=14	14x5	= 70
22	: 59	2x9=18	18-2=16	16x5	= 80
23	: 17	2x1=2	3+7=10	2x10	= 20
23	: 19	2x3=6	1+9=10	6x10	= 60
23	: 25	2+3=5	5x2=10	10x5	= 50
23	: 27	2x3=6	7-2=5	6x5	= 30
23	: 35	2x3=6	6x5=30	30x3	= 90
23	: 38	3+3=6	2x6=12	12+8	= 20
23	: 38	2x3=6	8-3=5	6x5	= 30
23	: 42		3+42=45	2x45	= 90
23	: 44	2+3=5	4+4=8	5x8	= 40
23	: 44	2+3=5	5x4=20	20x4	= 80
23	: 46	2x3=6	6+4=10	10x6	= 60
23	: 46	3x6=18	18x4=72	72-2	= 70
23	: 49	2x3=6	6+4=10	10x9	= 90
23	: 53	2x3=6	6x5=30	30x3	= 90
23	: 54		2x3=6	6+54	= 60
23	: 56	2+5=7	6/3=2	7+2	= 9
23	: 56	3x6=18	18-2=16	16x5	= 80
23	: 58	2x5=10	8-3=5	10x5	= 50
23	: 58	8/2=4	4x5=20	20x3	= 60
23	: 58	2x3=6	6+8=14	14x5	= 70
23	: 59	2x9=18	18-3=15	15x5	= 75
27	: 88	2x7=14	14+8=22	22+8	= 30
27	: 94	2x9=18	18+7=25	25x4	= 100
32	: 85	3x2=6	6+8=14	14x5	= 70
34	: 67	3x7=21	21x4=84	84+6	= 90
36	: 89	6+9=15	15/3=5	5x8	= 40
37	: 78	7+7=14	3x14=42	42+8	= 50
46	: 78	6+7=13	13x8=104	104-4	= 100
49	: 69	4x9=36	36/6=6	6x9	= 54
56	: 89	5x8=40	40x9=360	360/6	= 60
56	: 94	5x4=20	20x9=180	180/6	= 30
59	: 47	9+7=16	16/4=4	5x4	= 20
63	: 84	6x8=48	3x4=12	48+12	= 60
63	: 99	9x9=81	81-6=75	75/3	= 25
64	: 68	6+6=12	12x8=96	96+4	= 100
64	: 78	6+7=13	13x8=104	104-4	= 100
65	: 45	5x4=20	20-5=15	6x15	= 90
66	: 78	6+8=14	14x6=84	84+7	= 91
67	: 37	6+7=13	13+7=20	20x3	= 60
67	: 57	6+7=13	13+7=20	20x5	= 100
67	: 62	6+7=13	13+2=15	15x6	= 90
67	: 79	7+9=16	6x16=96	96-7	= 89
67	: 89	6+7=13	13+8=21	21+9	= 30
68	: 89	8x8=64	64x9=576	576/6	= 96
69	: 64	6x4=24	24-9=15	15x6	= 90
69	: 75	6+9=15	15x7=105	105-5	= 100
69	: 87	6+9=15	15+8=23	23+7	= 30
69	: 88	9x8=72	72/6=12	12+8	= 20
75	: 49	7+9=16	16/4=4	4x5	= 20
75	: 96	9+6=15	7x15=105	105-5	= 100
76	: 57	7+5=12	12x7=84	84+6	= 90
76	: 67	7+7=14	14x6=84	84+6	= 90
76	: 75	7+6=13	13+7=20	20x5	= 100
76	: 98	6+8=14	7x14=98	98-9	= 89
78	: 28	7+8=15	8-2=6	15x6	= 90
78	: 77	7+8=15	15x7=105	105-7	= 98
79	: 42	9x2=18	7+18=25	25x4	= 100
79	: 76	7+6=13	13x7=91	91-9	= 82
84	: 96	8-4=4	9+6=15	4x15	= 60
85	: 32	3x2=6	8+6=14	14x5	= 70
85	: 57	8+7=15	5x5=25	15+25	= 40
86	: 34	6x3=18	18x4=72	8+72	= 80
86	: 46	6x6=36	36/4=9	8+9	= 17
86	: 47	6+7=13	13x4=52	8+52	= 60
86	: 49	8-4=4	6+9=15	4x15	= 60
86	: 67	6+7=13	13x6=78	78-8	= 70
86	: 67	8x6=48	6x7=42	48+42	= 90
86	: 96	6+6=12	12x9=108	108-8	= 100
86	: 96	6+9=15	8x15=120	120/6	= 20
88	: 27	8x2=16	8x7=56	56-16	= 40
88	: 27	8-2=6	8+7=15	6x15	= 90
88	: 62	8+6=14	8x2=16	14+16	= 30
89	: 99	8x9=72	72-9=63	63/9	= 7
93	: 95	9x3=27	27-9=18	18x5	= 90
94	: 66	9+6=15	15x4=60	60/6	= 10
94	: 89	9+9=18	4x8=32	18+32	= 50
94	: 89	9+9=18	18x4=72	72+8	= 80
96	: 47	9+7=16	16x4=64	64+6	= 70
97	: 77	9x7=63	63+7=70	70/7	= 10
98	: 76	9x8=72	72/6=12	12+7	= 19
99	: 99	9x9=81	81-9=72	72/9	= 8

WWW.MENTALCLOCK.COM